RAISE A NATION

REVOLUTIONIZING THE BLACK COMMUNITY

Cedric L. Davis

"If You are Black, then You should be thinking Black, and if You are not thinking Black at this late date. I feel sorry for You."

-Malcom X

Table Of Contents

DEDICATION

To the Black community as a whole, to the crying grieving mothers, grandmothers, wives, sisters, and children who have been left behind due to unnecessary violence.

To the countless souls of the young men, women and children who have been lost to senseless violence.

To the children of this generation and future generations. Know and believe that you are the change. You
are the future.
Special dedication to my grandchildren, Javiar, Khaliah, Vonte, and my baby princess Londyn K.

Sincerely and dutifully,

Cedric L. Davis

"If we want to lead the people, we must not be out of their sight."

-Sojourner Truth

THANKS

Thanks to my children. Ya'll are my motivation. I love all of you dearly.

Special thanks to MY grandsons, Braylyn and Javiar. This is definitely for you guys.

"Give to the world your best, and the best will come back to you."

-Issa Rae

INTRODUCTION

*"I know where I'm going, and
I know the truth, and I don't have to be what you
want me
to be. I'm free to be what I want."*

-Muhammad Ali

This is my diatribe. Some may agree; some may not, but the fact that a change is a must in the Black community, and in the thinking and actions of Black people, cannot be denied.

Revolutionize means to change fundamentally or completely. A complete emotional, mental, economic, and spiritual change. This is what the Black community needs.

This is no religious book, but God's wisdom has to be strongly considered, referenced and followed. God told Abraham, "Know certainly that your descendants will be strangers in a land that is not theirs, and will serve them, and they will afflict them four hundred years. (1619-2017) and also the nation whom they serve I will judge; afterward they will come out with great possessions" (Genesis 15:13-14).

The time to come out is now. God was talking to Abraham about Israel, but today, this word is for Black nations in America.

I am no prophet, but I am told that history repeats itself, and a blind man can see that the time of our oppression has come to its end. We are a resilient people, and there is no mountain too high, valley too low, or water too deep that we can't conquer if we come together and stick together as a people and use the knowledge and wisdom given to us by our creator.

When the children of Israel were being oppressed in Egypt, God drew Moses from among them to lead the people to freedom and to change. "Their cry came up to God because of the bondage. I have surely seen the oppression of my people. Come now therefore, and I will send you that you may bring my people out" (Exodus 2:23, 3:7-10).

God has heard the cries of the mothers, grandmothers, children, and fathers who have lost loved ones, and so have you and I. Too many! We feel the heartache and pain. God is drawing out men and women who believe in the power and strength that was given to us as a people. We must tap into it and use it for the betterment and advancement of our people.

Believing is not enough. To do this work of bringing about change, revolutionizing the Black community, one has to be willing to tap into that power and wisdom to go on the journey. This is not a job for just one person; it is for the people as a whole. When Moses led the Israelites out of Egypt, they all came out. Even so, we the Black nation must also all come out as one.

It takes a nation to raise a nation. When Jesus sent the disciples out to bring change, He sent them out in pairs. Moses had the seventy elders, and they were all on one accord. Therefore, we must also be on one accord.

Sure, we will have different ideas on how to reach the needed change, and that is okay as long as our end goal is the same. (To make our communities safer, to educate our children, to grow economically, to gain a political stronghold, to ultimately elevate our whole nation of people.)

How do we reach that destination? We put God at the head and keep Him in our midst. We go forward in faith. This is our Red Sea!

It is time for that change! It is time to raise a nation and revolutionize the BLACK COMMUNITY.

MANHOOD

Train up a child in the way he should go, and when he is

old he will not depart from it.

-Proverbs 22:6

Why is it that young Black males associate manhood with physical dominance, machismo, and the sexual conquering of females? This is an absurd idea of manhood, but it is to no fault of their own.

The first and most inherent thing we should teach our young boys is who they are and what faith in God and believing in themselves means in their daily lives.

Training is the repetitive action of showing through example how they can be better men than we have been. The objective is to teach good moral values and to build character, which is a substantial part of the training and upbringing of the manchild.

If you ever played a sport, were in a band, or were on any type of team or weight trained, then you know what it means to train. Training is the key component to becoming better at something, maybe even perfecting it. So, what are we, Black men, doing to train our manchild, to prepare him for manhood?

Other cultures have things that men do with the manchild in preparation for manhood. These events are not sprung on the manchild. They are trained for this day from the time they were babies. Training and preparation is continuous throughout their upbringing. After the rite of passage is complete, the manchild is ushered into manhood with a sense of pride and an experience that he will never forget.

In Western Kenya, the manchild from the Bukusu tribe between the tender ages of 10 and 14 goes through an age-old ritual of circumcision, in which he ceremonially becomes a man. Every manchild who completes the ritual is bound in brotherhood (bakoki) to the men who have helped to usher him into manhood, and rightly so. In his village and tribe, he is no longer a manchild; he is a man now. The men of the village build him his own hut. He no longer lives with his parents or sits with them at meals; he now can choose what he wants to eat, instead of eating what he is told. Now that he is a man, and no longer a manchild, he is accountable as a man and has responsibilities that are expected to be carried out as a man in the tribe and village.

Some cultures teach the manchild combat tactics to prepare them for military service when they reach Manhood, as they do in the Ukraine.

In some countries, young boys and girls are forced to become child combat soldiers. The child who is exposed to this life never even has the chance to be a child, much less to be trained to become a man.

In the Jewish culture, the manchild is taught and trained up to the age of 13 years old, readying him for his rite of passage into manhood. The ritual is called a bar mitzvah. This ritual performed by Jewish men commemorates the age when a manchild becomes accountable for his own sins and actions. He is now a man!

In places like England's Pacific Trobriand Islands, pubescent boys leave their family to join a group house and to be tutored by a maternal uncle, to show respect for ancestry and a commitment to the community. Boys of the Kpelle tribe in Liberia are secluded for four years for initiations, instructions and ritual circumcisions, and in some southern cultures, young boys are trained to work hard for their families, and this is what ultimately turns them into men.

There is never enough that we can do, yet there is never enough that we can't do in training up the Black manchild for manhood.

White men in America train their young boys to hunt with guns and bows and arrows. They teach them to dress game in the fields. They teach them how to survive in the event of a natural disaster or when lost in the wilderness. If they own businesses, or whatever profession they work in, they groom their children for success in that trade whether they go into it or not. This is all in preparation for manhood.

So, what exactly are we, the Black men in America, doing to prepare our children for manhood? I think it would be safe to say that in today's times, less than 15% of young Black males know how to hunt and dress game, and they would be lost in the wilderness; they would not know what to do in a house fire or in a natural disaster. Once again, this is not their fault; it is the fault of us Black men and fathers. We are not being held accountable in the home and in the com-munity for our responsibilities as teachers, mentors, leaders, trainers and fathers of young Black males. Surely, we don't expect the women to do it all!

We are to be the examples of integrity, magnanimity, dexterity, character, moral values, intelligence, hard work, and success that is conducive in developing the next generation of Black men, steadily advancing as a community, people, and nation.

Yes, Black people in America have suffered some long hard years. There were 266 years of physical slavery, from 1619 to 1865. These were years of torture and the family unit was divested and emasculated. The Black man's role as protector and provider stripped away from him. Then there was the one hun -dred or so years of reconstruction and Jim Crow seg -regation from 1866 to the late 1960s. Through our re -siliency, we have not only survived, but we have come back stronger. Yet now we are our greatest enemy.

History is a great thing to reflect on and move on from. We should never forget, but we tend to lose focus on what lies ahead while watching the rear-view mirror. Many of us know that we come from kings, emperors, princes, queens, empresses, and princesses, and our ancestors cultivated and civilized nations. This is wonderful information, but if generations of the Black race do not know who, what, and where they have come from, then how will they ever know where they can go? They feel hopeless, so we must give them hope.

"Train up a child in the way that he should go, and when he is old, he will not depart from it." This is, to every Black man, a command, not a suggestion. It doesn't matter if you have your own children or not.

We have to be active in training. Due to our failure to take an active role, we have allowed all this specious propaganda into our homes, and it is destroying our communities. *I say, no more!*

If we continue to allow the mendacious idealism of entertainment and social media to distract us from the reality of what is happening in our communities, we'll soon wake up back in 1712.

Many of us may not live to see the complete change, but we have children, grandchildren, and so on. Why don't we put the work in for them?

It is now or Never! If you are a man reading this, are you ready? Are you willing to make whatever sacrifices necessary to help train up the manchild and prepare him for manhood? Show them good moral values, character, integrity and how to be dedicated to the educating, strengthening and protecting of the tribe, the village, the Black community, and the Black nation.

Every Black neighborhood in America is a village, and each family is a tribe. All these separately make up the Black community as a whole, and if in no other way, here we are connected as one.

To my sisters, queens and mothers reading this book:

There is no doubt in my mind that you are ready to see us Black men step up and take the bull by the horns and ride it down. You are ready to see us regain control of the manchild, of our homes and communities. You are ready for us to be the living, breathing examples of honest, respectful, courageous, hard-working, driven, creative, successful men our sons can look up to and emulate.

We cannot talk the manchild into Manhood. We have to walk, guide and lead them there.

REAL NIGGAISM

"Take the case of the wild, stud horse... compare the breaking process with two captured nigger males in their

natural state (uncivilized savages)..."

-Willie Lynch

The Making of a Slave

Real nigga! I hear it proclaimed proudly all the time. "I'm a real nigga," or real niggas do this or that. "I been a real nigga my whole life." At a time in my life, this was funny and cool, but now it is disturbing; it is absurd.

Look at how this slave owner described a nigger. He said that a nigger in his "Natural state" is an "uncivilized savage," then he goes on and compares him to an animal, a wild horse that needs to be broken.

I will not elaborate on the atrocious breaking of a slave Lynch describes in his letter. If you want to know more, google "The Making of a Slave by Willie Lynch." What I propose to do is deter my young brothers from referring to themselves or one another as niggas or real niggas.

This has become such a norm that not only are Black males calling themselves real niggas, but you have some Black females, White males\females, Mexicans, Puerto Ricans, and Asians claiming to be real niggas too.

I've even heard Black females say, "I don't want nothing but a real nigga!" What type of female would proclaim that?

Why would any Black person in America want to be called a real nigga or a nigger period? Ignorance! My people perish from a lack of knowledge and from being led astray by rap music and movies. The first time being a real nigga was publicly put in a song or movie and there was no outrage and no cry of disgust by the Black community, like the plague, it began to spread and now is an infestation of the mind.

I ain't going to lie; at one point in my life, I was stupid enough to call myself a nigga and I tried to act out being a real nigga. That didn't work out too well for me. Look where I have spent the past 13 years (prison). I came into the knowledge of self and the weight that word has and how it is affecting my people. I have almost erased this word from my vocabulary.

Now, I call myself a man, and I think and act as one, because I am a man. I will not be called a nigger by anyone, real or otherwise.

When we hear people, especially young Black males, refer to themselves as real niggas. It is not a term of endearment; it is a mind state. Being called a nigger by Whites means to them that you are an uncivilized savage, stupid, an animal, not even a man. Sadly in these days and times, it seems that young Black males who call themselves real niggas are actually trying to live up to being uncivilized savages, stupid, animals, and the characterization of being a nigger.

Prayerfully, we can all together encourage our young people to see themselves for who they really are, and we can assist them in becoming the best person they can be.

The word nigger has actually been taken out of context. It is derived from the African country Niger or the Niger River, of which means black or dark. Just as Negro is derived from the Spanish word negra, which means black. To be Black is to be proud! Ya'll know they hate on us.

In ancient Ethiopia, the word was not nigger but negus, which means emperor or king, and negusi to mean empress or queen. In ancient Egypt, the spelling was quite different: NGR. This also meant king. The title used in its proper context in ancient Africa and Egypt was a token of esteem. The European or White slave owners took the title, changed its spelling, and started using it to degrade, belittle, and defame our people to foster hatred amongst our ancestors, their offspring, and us, to this day.

This ain't about race! Then again, it is. This is about how we have come to accept something that has been in the past, throughout history, and is still used today to negatively describe us as a people. We have embraced this title as a badge of honor, but in reality, we are only denigrating ourselves. This term has not been turned from a negative to a positive, especially when our actions create the content of what it means to be a real nigga.

If, when people label themselves as real niggas, they emulate the life, style, dignity, intelligence, and charisma of kings and queens, it may be tolerable, but that ain't the case now, is it? From what I have seen and heard, to be a real nigga means:

*You are cutthroat, out for self, but you will play close just to get in position.

*You don't tell what kind of chemical (drug) you use. Real niggas stay geeked out of their minds.

*You will lie, cheat and steal from your own family just to get what you want.

*You will murder your best friend, act like you didn't, and comfort his mother and family.

*If it doesn't benefit you, you could care less.

*You neglect your children; you will take food from their mouths just to satisfy your own needs.

*You think it's cool being dumb; you can barely spell your own child's name.

*You think that a nice looking, well-shaped, uneducated female with no future plans is a dime.

*You believe you can sell dope forever because you don't want to work.

*You'd rather waste all your money on Jordans, jerseys, clothes, and cars while you live off mama or off your babymama.

*You hate yourself and kind.

*You'll fight, shoot, and kill your own people for the simplest thing, but you will not stand for a righteous cause.

*You leave your family to fend for themselves.

*While in prison, you get into sexual relationships with other men, then you get out on the street and act like you never did it.

*You don't want to get out of prison because that means responsibility; you would have to take care of yourself.

There is so much negativity associated with the real nigga ideology. It is sad and troubling, so it's time for its demolition. We can in no way allow ourselves or our children to be commensurate with the unintelligent idea of real niggaism. We have to completely disassociate with that mentality. The word nigga must be erased from our vocabularies. We should not allow it to be spoken in our homes, cars, or communities. We must educate our children as to its meaning and its effect on our ancestors, us, and our history.

It's time that we extricate our youth from this real nigga idiocy. This mindset is detrimental to our growth and advancement as well as to our unity. It has a damaging effect on our youth, and on our young men in particular. Change will only come when we are all ready. George Jackson said, "It is the worst form of niggaism to hook, stab, cut, and jab other Blacks." Sadly, we do this daily in words and deeds.

That being true, why do we do it and when will we stop? Real niggaism is a deadly poison, and being Black does not make you a nigga. We are only who we believe ourselves to be.

GANGSTAISM

*"We were alienated from our sources, isolated, and
remolded*

to fit a certain form, to fill a specific purpose. No

consideration was or has ever been given to our

being anything other than what we

were originally intended to be."

-George Jackson

Gangstaism, like niggaism, is a fruitless idiotic mindset that is detrimental to our progress as a race of people. When young Black males have this sinister ideal of gangstaism, it emasculates them individually and gives them a false sense of unity. Every young person wants to fit in and belong, be noticed, have a name, and have a reputation in the hood. Yet that name or reputation does not have to be negative.

Seven out of ten young Black males associate themselves to some sort of gang or organization. To take part in these gangs or organizations, or to call oneself a gangsta, they have to have a certain demeanor. They have to act tough, be fearless, talk violent, and be violent if they want to claim to be a gangsta.

Who exactly does all this gangstaism affect? The truth is that it destroys the lives of our children. It disrupts our homes, our schools, and our communities, and it keeps the tears and fears flowing in the eyes of mothers and children, and it incites fear in society.

Gangstaism is a regressive attitude. How is it that we have allowed our children to become so emotionally detached? Is it that we have forgotten how to love, so we have fallen short in teaching our children what it means to love another? Over the past forty years, this gangstaism or gangsta mentality has been festering. It has completely infected the minds of our youth, and it must be destroyed. God and a sense of spirituality has to be reintroduced into our children's psyche. We have taken our focus and trust off of God and placed it in image and material things. The pseudo-promise of fast money, fine living, and social status has corrupted our minds.

If gangstaism is portraying a tough image, then who are we feigning toughness to? The government, the police, corporate America? Trust me, they are not afraid. Why, because we are not harming them; we are hurting us, and they are capitalizing on our self-destruction. We are our own worst enemy.

Blacks have been brainwashed by movies such as *The Mack, Superfly, Colors, Menace to Society, Boys N Da Hood, Juice, Set It Off*, and by gangsta music and the way in which we are depicted by the media. When the assimilating of gangstaism began, we should have put an end to it. It was an illusion that we were sold for our own destruction and degradation. The music and movies that were elevating and educating us re-ceived very little attention while gangsta stuff was well promoted. The plan has always been to keep us re-pressed, " remodeled to fit into certain forms, to fill a certain purpose."

Here is an example of the apathetic mentality of gangstaism and how it has no regard for others' feelings or for how it affects the lives of others.

There was this guy, we'll call him Slim. Now, this is a true story. Slim has been incarcerated for close to ten years. He has a fourteen-year-old daughter, a ten-year-old son, and his mother, whom the children live with, is a very sickly woman. The children's biological mother died some time ago, so Slim and his sick mother are all the children have. Slim's mother sends him $75 a month, but because Slim is in segregation, he has to have someone call his mom to get the money for him.

So, a guy had been calling and getting the money for Slim for months. He had always handled his business with Slim, so they were always good until this one month when the guy did not come through for Slim.

From what Slim tells me, in every phone call and in every letter he gets from his mom and children, they are pouring out their hearts to him, crying and telling him how much they love him, how much they want and need him to come home. Slim said that he wants to go home and that he loves his family very much. But Slim has a problem: he thinks he is a gangsta.

Slim and I had this conversation in November, and Slim has a parole review in March. There is a possibility that he could make parole. But that is no longer his concern. He has to get that money or just try and prove some point.

Slim told his mother what happened with the money. When he told her, she said to him, "Don't worry about that; I'll send you some more, just come home. That money ain't nothing. I need you home; these children need their daddy." The children also pleaded with him. Remember, their mother is deceased, so Slim is the only surviving parent they have. God forbid, if Slim's mother were to pass away, these children would be all alone in this world.

None of this mattered to Slim. He thought he was a gangsta, so he had to uphold his reputation at all costs, whether freedom or death.

With parole on the line and his children needing him to come home, and with his mom sick and dying, this is what Slim had to say about it all: "Man, I have been in prison almost ten years. Ain't nobody ever took nothing from me, so I can't let that go. Soon as I see that dude, I'm shooting on site (meaning, he is going to stab the guy). Ain't nobody ever took nothing and ain't nobody gonna take nothing from me and get away with it." Now comes the justification as to why Slim has to react with violence.

"That's my momma's money. I don't play with my momma's money."

"Didn't your momma say not to worry about it and to come home?" I asked.

"Yeah, but she don't understand. I ain't no punk." (His words were much harsher and vulgar.)

"Well, what about your kids and parole?"

"Look, bra, you know I can't let that go. Nobody ever took nothing from me since I been in prison, and I ain't bout to let it start now."

Before I ended the conversation, I wanted to leave Slim with something to think about, so I asked him, "Slim, what is most important to you: staying in prison and being a prison gangsta or being free at home and being a father and taking care of your mother? They need you! Your absence is causing them to suffer. Think about it."

Most young Black males not only talk like this, but they actually think and act or try to act out what they talk about. This is one of the main reasons there is so much violence among Black youths. They feel they have a point to prove and an image to uphold or a reputation to build.

It is time to change course. We are losing our future; we are losing our babies younger and faster. Raising a gangsta only fills graves and cells while emptying homes, communities and hearts.

By changing what goes into the minds of our children, we change what comes out of them. In this way, we start REVOLUTIONIZING THE BLACK COMMUNITY and RAISING UP OUR NATION.

THE BLACK WOMAN

"The Black woman has in the past few hundred
years
been the only force holding us together and holding
us up."

-George Jackson

This is a profound statement. The brother goes on to say, "The Black woman has absorbed the biggest part of their many shocks and strains of existence under the slave order." This was said by George Jackson over fifty years ago, and it still rings true.

Black women are the crown jewels, the strength, the driving forces behind the Black family and the Black Nation.

The Black women in my life whom God blessed me with as influences include my late grandmothers

Mrs. Catherine Johnson Davis and Mrs. Bertha Bruce, my adoptive mother Mrs. Cathyrn Lockett, my biological mother Mrs. Marita Davis Brown, and all my aunts who were and many still are the strength and guiding light of our family.

Black women are some of the most highly educated college women in America. They are our mothers, wives, sisters, daughters, and the nurturers of our children. Black women of today are CEOs of large companies, small businesses owners, doctors, judges and senators. They are the pride of the Black race; at least this is what I know to be true. Above all this, Black women can work a long hard day and still come home take care of the kids, cook dinner and love on their mate.

Knowing how important the Black woman is and her true worth, why do we Black men not show our Black women, our Black queens, the love, respect, honor, and dedication they deserve? We have failed them through the idiotic ideology, false propaganda and advertisements of music, movies and mass media. We buy into the illusions, and then we start disrespecting our women. We have failed to protect, love and support our Black women.

Queens, empresses, and rulers of nations are what our Black women are, like Queen Hatshepsut of Africa, Queen Nefertiti in Egypt. There was also the

Warrior-Queen of Ethiopia and Saba in Southern Arabia. The Queen whom King Solomon, the son of King David, spoke of in the Bible (they called her Queen Sheba or Queen of Sheba) and loved dearly. They also had a son whose name was Menelik.

Even today, here in America, Black women have the same spirit and skill as those ancient queens, to rule and to cultivate nations. They rule wherever they are. They are still modern-day queens.

Nevertheless, Black Queens need Black Kings, but it seems that we, Black men, are afraid to take on that responsibility.

Look into the Black communities, the projects, and neighborhoods of Black families, and what do you see? You see Black queens struggling but juggling alone. They are working, hustling, paying bills, taking care of our children, and running businesses. These are the women we have abandoned and left to rule alone.

I salute every Black woman! They are God's gift to us. When things seem to be falling apart, instead of giving up, they look to God as their one true help. They find that strength inside of themselves, and God provides the sustenance they need. He sends other Black women to encourage and comfort them. The coolest thing is that in a crisis situation, Black women always come together. Why is this? Because they all are or have experienced the same or similar struggles; it's in their make-up to look to one another because the man has been absent.

Where would we be as a nation without the influence, courage, hard work, and sacrifice of the Black woman? I don't know the answer, and I don't even want to think on it. What I can tell you is this: we would be in much worse shape today if it were not for the Black women of history and today.

God, as the Bible tells us, created woman as a helper for man. God knew what he was doing. The Black woman has not only been a helper, but she has carried the Black race on her back and is still carrying us today.

Looking around the nation, what do you see when there is an injustice in the Black community? The Black woman is first to stand up and speak up, voicing her concerns. When we see protests and rallies, there are more Black women leading and participating than men. This should not be so, but it is a sad reality.

Black men are supposed to support and protect our women but instead, they are standing up for, protecting, and supporting us. Even worse is the fact that Black males are becoming so violent and unpredictable that Black women are beginning to fear them.

This should never be so! It is a bad sign when Black women are afraid of Black men, who are the very people Black women should always feel safe with.

In the days of my youth, my mom would run us outside to play. We'd stay out there all day. Not so in these days and times. Black women are afraid to let their babies play outside for fear that they may be shot by a stray bullet. This will change, but only when Black men and the community as a whole begin to restore that sense of confidence and the feelings of love and security they once knew.

Black women are intelligent, resourceful, loving, stern, and full of pride. Their pride is not arrogance; it is a humble pride. Most of the ones I have known are respectful and respected in their communities.

Respect is a serious thing to Black women. I remember as a child my mom would say to me, "I don't care if the person is a drunk bum on a corner, it better not ever reach my ears that you was disrespectful, to any adult, do you hear me?" Oh, you bet I heard. When she said something, you knew that it was the law, and her actions reflected the same. You'd never see my mom be disrespectful to anyone, not even in the heat of the moment. I tell you what, though, she sure could set someone straight with a few words and a very serious look. My mom made sure that we got to

Sunday school every Sunday and that we had something to put in the collection plate.

Many of the Black women from my childhood were not highly educated, but they articulated what they wanted to say and doled out wisdom. Just as it was said of Sojourner Truth, they were strong on faith and could out-work most men in the field. This is also true of the majority of today's Black women; they are passionate, strong, and full of fire.

Might I include another truth here? Black women are the most beautiful, attractive, and sexy beings that God ever created. They need never to try to live up to the Euro-American standard of beauty. They have natural beauty and sex appeal. All they have to do is look to our ancestors, who were the quintessence of beauty. Queen Nefertiti's name means "the beautiful one has come." Her beauty is still spoken of today, and Queen Makeda was also called "Makeda the beautiful." Both these women were naturally beautiful.

What about the Black women of the 60s, 70s and 80s, like Angela Davis, Pam Grier, Chaka Khan, Diana Ross, Yo Mama and my mama. All these beautiful women rocked afros and little to no make-up. They were smoking hot. Just look at how they age so gracefully, and how they maintain all their curves and still eat what they want. They don't need all that superficial mess.

The younger generation of Black women are becoming more atavistic. Losing the make-up and wearing their natural hair. Women like Danai Gurira, Lupita Nyongo, Issa Rae, and Marlene Barnett, just to name a few beautiful sisters rocking that natural look.

The time has gone past that us Black men need to appreciate the beauty, strength, and intelligence of our Black women. Although, many already know how beautiful and smart they are, we still need to encourage them to love the skin they are in,

Furthermore, our daughters will grow up to be beautiful Black women. They will know their worth by the examples we set in honoring, respecting, loving, guiding, and encouraging them and the Black women in and around our lives. They will watch the women in their lives who are their initial role models. They will absorb every action and every word. So, our job is to set the best living examples to be followed and passed down from generation to generation. Change starts with self. Our actions affect their future. So, my beautiful Black queens, learn to love you, respect yourself and demand respect from all others. Know that you are very intelligent and that you are the most beautiful beings God has created. Love the skin, hair, shape, and style that is all yours, and teach the next generation of little Black queens that they too are beautiful and unique.

FATHERHOOD

"I see the Black family unit is in ruins...the family unit was destroyed

during chattel slavery. Men had the sense of family responsibility trained out of them. It is our first and basic weakness."

-George Jackson

Becoming a father is one of the most awesome, emotional, thought-provoking, and fear-filled events that a man will ever experience. Fatherhood is a mindset, and when a man becomes a father, it is the most important job and the greatest role he will ever have in his life. From the moment his child is born or from the moment he assumes the role of a father, everything he says and does or does not do will shape and mold his child's life.

"A father," as I wrote in my first book, *Breaking Da Cycle: Keeping Our Youth Alive and Out of Prison,* "should be the first man his daughter falls in love with." Her first boy crush should be a dad crush.

Our actions as fathers, the way in which we show affection or interact with our mothers, wives and daughters will be very conducive as to how our daughters view men. Eight times out of ten, our interactions with family, the love, devotion and respect we give as fathers will be a deciding factor in the type of man, husband, and companion they will seek to father their children. Girls learn from their fathers or the men in their lives what to look for in a man as they grow. Therefore, we must try hard to be the best example we can possibly be.

We fathers play an even greater role in the lives, growth and development of our sons, especially on a mental level. Boys more than likely try to emulate their father's every action. Even if the father is not a physical presence in their lives, what they hear about their father is what they will try to live up to in some way, whether the father was violent, abusive, a gangsta, whatever. Even if the son chooses a different lifestyle, he will carry some of those traits. By knowing this, we cannot be latent fathers, but we must be dedicated to being the best teachers, trainers, and listeners in life to our children in a family setting.

It is a father's inherent duty to ensure that we teach our children, especially our son's, basic life skills, such as personal hygiene, self-grooming, style, minor car repair, home maintenance, lawn care, gardening, cooking, etc. Also, teaching them respect and love for community is important, how to work hard but smart, and most of all, dedication to family. These things and more are what our sons must look to us as fathers for, to know how to conduct themselves when they become men and fathers.

Back in 2007, after my then 22-year-old brother James was killed, I was told a lot about how my oldest son Lacedric, who was around 10 or 11 years old when James was killed, was acting. He looked up to James. My son is 20 years old now, but at the time, I was told that he would always say how he wanted to be like me, his dad, who had been in prison since he was 7, and like his uncle James, who had just gotten killed, shot seven times and left in the middle of the street like an animal.

I was proud to hear that my son wanted to be like me, but at the same time, I was scared. There was no way that I could or would allow that idea to bloom into a reality in my son's life. I am his father, and he is my responsibility whether I am in prison or not, and I couldn't let what happened to me and James happen to him. I stayed in his ear, drilling into his head and heart my love for him. I told him how being like James and being like me was not a good idea. I told him I believed in him and wanted him to be much better than me. I had to constantly encourage him to be his best, and I must admit, there were some trying times, but God has kept my boy safe and on the right track. So far, he is doing fine.

Not only was there my oldest son for me to guide to do the right things but I have two daughters, Mercedes and Kamelia, and three other sons Lajohn (AKA Tra), Tyler and Tariq to think of. Being incarcerated for the past 13 years and not being a physical presence in my children's lives has not stopped me from being the best father and example that I could be to them. I was constantly reminding them of what I expect of them, reassuring them of how much I love them and believe in them.

My oldest daughter, of whom I am so proud of, Mercedes, has graduated high school, Class of 2017, and is now looking into ways to start her own business and maybe get into real estate. I am encouraging my other four kids to push on to that next level in life.

We Black fathers have been derelict in that duty long enough. The time has come that we step back into our roles as leaders in the family unit. Our beautiful Black women, who are our backbones, are the helpers God created to help us, and they need our help now. Being a father is not easy; it is a hard job and not for the timid or faint of heart. We have to look to God for guidance, patience, knowledge and wisdom to be good fathers. God is the only perfect father, but perfection is not the key. What is needed is that we pour out our hearts, give all we have to teach, love, protect, communicate, and usher our children into and through each stage of their lives. We are the captains of this ship, and it is our duty to navigate the course to our children's future.

If you, the reader, were raised like me without a father (I never knew my father and still don't) in your life, you know firsthand the adverse effect it has played in determining who we are today. The absence of a father is, in my opinion, more detrimental to boys than girls. The lack of fathers or father figures, if we are completely honest, is the reason for the degeneration and destruction of the Black family, the community and our sons.

The Bible tells us, "You fathers, do not provoke your children to wrath, but bring them up in the training and admonition of the Lord" (Ephesians 6:4). How can this be done when fathers are not there? If there, how can it be done if they are condescending?

Being a father is a joy that not all men get to experience. "Children's children are the crown of old men, and the glory of children is their father" (Proverbs 17:6).

Children are a blessing from God. Black men must be held accountable as fathers. We should be honored to teach our children the knowledge of God, knowledge of self and kindness. When we get back to our rightful place and take full responsibility for ourselves, our families, and our communities, we will see the needed changes in our society. Our rightful place in the family and community cannot be denied us, but the choice not to take it is ours, and that choice is not profitable to us as a people. Fathers must make the right choice.

"The harvest is ripe, but the workers are few." The change will be subtle, but there is no doubt that change must come, and soon. How exactly does it come? Through us fathers, with our innate ability to be leaders, to be examples of faithful devotion in the care and defense of our families, respecting our women, encouraging, empowering, and educating our children and leading our families and communities.

God has been sympathetic toward us for so long. I for one am so thankful for His Mercy.

When a father is a loving, guiding, presence in a child's life, it makes all the difference in the world. So, why don't you and I be that presence in some child's life, even if we don't have our own children. We can help raise them so they can raise up our nation and bring love, peace, and unity to strengthen the Black family unit.

70% of Black children in America are without fathers; let's see if we can change that. Surely, we can!

BLACK-ON-BLACK VIOLENCE

"I am a victim, born innocent, a total product of my surroundings.

Everything that I am, I developed into because of circumstantial and

situational pressures. I was born knowing nothing; necessity and environment formed me and everyone like me."

-George Jackson

Looking at the rate in which young Black males commit crimes of violence against one another should make us stop and dissect what is happening to us and around us. The opening excerpt written in a letter by Brother George Jackson back in 1967 resonates on our youth still in 2016. If we actually think about it, the violence that our children learn does not come directly from inside the home. Society plays a major role in their psychological development.

The violence our children learn from movies, music, their peers and the environment is poisoning their minds. This poison is deliberately administered as a subtle tactic used by a capitalistic society to maintain its dominance over a nation of people.

When poison is disguised by mixing it in food or drink, it does not change its poisonous nature. In this fashion, the poison is more dangerous because in its present state of incognito, it can be ingested unknowingly. This method conjoined with falsehoods and half-truths has been used to mislead and to turn Black males toward violence and hatred for themselves.

Video games contribute heavily to the influence of violence. Young Black males are belittled, shamed, bullied, taken advantage of, and called weak if they show any signs of fear or timidity. Resentment forms and they begin to gravitate more toward a violent character in order to fit in, to be accepted, and to have a name and a reputation. The result of that is the violence, murders, robberies, and assaults we see committed in the Black communities all around the nation.

As the violence surges in the streets between young Black males, where 95% of it is Black-on-Black violence among Black men in prison has surged also. For the past sixteen years here in the Alabama Department of Corrections, 90% of the violence has been Black-on-Black. As a matter of fact, just four days ago, some Black males at Stanton Correctional got into an altercation that left a brother dead and two families were torn apart. Just the thought of this causes me depression, coupled with the fact that it seems most of our people don't seem to care about what's happening to us. Oh, how I wish that this were not so. Angela Davis said," Jails and prisons are designed to break the human being, to convert the population to specimens in a zoo—obedient to our keepers but dangerous to each other." What a true statement. Prison also causes the majority of Black men, especially the younger ones who experience it, to become very apathetic. That in turn contributes to the Black-on Black violence in the streets.

In the thirteen years that I have been incarcerated, I have witnessed Black men stab, rob, rape (I never actually saw a rape, but I did see an attempt and heard stories), steal from, gang up and beat mercilessly on one another. This has not happened in just one facility; it happens all over the state and all over the country. The administration in here, just as the administration on the outside, promotes violence among Blacks. There has been numerous murders here in prison over the years, Black on Black, and I have witnessed quite a few of them. When Black men are found dead in their cells, there is no real investigation; it's business as usual. Nothing changes, life goes on, and most times, no one is charged for the crime.

When and where did we learn to hate ourselves so much? We go out of our way to destroy our own kind.

On August 27, 2016, I was listening to the news on the radio. In a Black neighborhood in Birmingham, Alabama, a precious four-year-old beautiful Black child was shot and killed. Why? Because two young misguided Black males had an argument over a cellphone. Can you believe it? These two young Black brothers could not resolve a simple disagreement without it turning to violence and shots being fired. Just look at who was affected by this nonsense. Rodriguez Ferguson's life, which had just begun, ended all of a sudden. His mother was grief-stricken by the loss of her baby. Because of someone's stupidity and careless act, she will never be able to hug, kiss and watch her child grow up. How many more mothers have experienced this?

This senseless violence affects the entire Black community, and it must be stopped.

Rest easy, little Rodriguez. I will never forget you, although I never met you.

I am pretty sure that one , if not both, of the young men involved in this tragic incident has gone to prison or some juvenile institution or they are acquainted with someone who has been to prison. Why could they not resolve a simple conflict without it resulting to violence and the loss of life? To do that, to be civilized, rational, to talk like men isn't gangsta. Real niggas don't do no talking! That's pie! These boys are taught in the streets and in the institutions about verbal altercations in which names are called and aggression is shown. If they don't address it right then and there by fighting, stabbing, or shooting, they are weak because they allowed someone to put down on them and disrespect them without doing anything about it. They are taught that if they ain't no killer, ain't no real shooter, then they ain't no real niggas, and they sho ain't gangsta.

How stupid is that mindset?

Every opportunity that presents itself to me to talk to a young man, Black, White or other but especially Black, I try to get them to see just how this way of thinking is destroying us as a people and causing a divide between us. We should be coming together, not falling farther apart.

There was an incident again in Birmingham, where some young men shot into a house hitting a little six-year-old girl in the back while she slept on her grandmother's couch. She survived, but what about the psychological trauma this will cause her? She was in a place where she should always feel safe, but will she feel safe now? Then there was an incident where someone shot into a car and hit a little boy in the leg. We have to protect our children and give them the chance to grow. They are our future; without them, our race will be eliminated.

When I was a small child, we stayed outside. Our parents would have to make us come inside. Not these days! Mothers are afraid to let their babies play outside for fear they may catch a stray bullet. Who can blame them? When are we going to bring peace back to the hood?

The violence that is in cartoons, movies, video games, music, schools and neighborhoods is being trained into our children. They are not born violent. How do we counter this? Stop allowing children to indulge in the violence! Don't buy the games, music, movies, or anything that promotes violence or self-destruction.

We don't have to support violent rap, movies, or games. Look at all the rappers that are chart toppers, such as Drake, Kendrick Lamar, and Kanye; their music is not violent. To say you can't make money unless the music is violent is bull!

Whites, Latinos, and Asians don't promote violence toward their own people, and they sure aren't degrading their women in music.

We need to stand together against these senseless killings. That means that we police our own communities, set boundaries, make rules and enforce them. If you commit an act of violence in one of our neighborhoods or communities, we will not protect you or act as if nothing has happened. We will make sure you are taken off of the streets, and if you can't or don't want to be rehabilitated over time, then we will exile you from our communities if need be.

It is important that we love our children just as God loved us, and that we teach them to love themselves and their own kind. We don't want them filling up the prisons and graveyards, as they are doing now, robbing and killing one another like they are in the Wild West.

Young Black children in particular must be taught that violence is not the solution to conflict. It does not make them real nigga or gangsta to help destroy or degrade themselves and their people. Teach them to debate responsibility and to resolve conflict peacefully. It has to be imbedded in their minds that this is the way the real world works; no one gets everything they want when they want it, and words will not kill them.

I loved my grandmother, God rest her soul. When we were kids, and there were a lot of us, we'd run to her after we started arguing and calling one another names. It'd get to where one or the other could not take it. We'd run to Mudea, crying. "Mu, he talkin' bout me." We would just cry but Mu always said, "Hush that fuss now; what you crying for? You ain't dead, is ya? Stop all that crying; words ain't gonna kill ya. Now go on back and play. Hush all that fuss. Mudea loves you." That would do it, and we'd be back at it, playing and laughing.

Mudea was always right. Those words never killed me or anyone else.

I don't know how you feel, but I am tired of hearing the stories, seeing it on the news, listening to the crying from mothers and families. I have been told and have now learned that when a person gets tired of something, they act on it to change what they are tired of. Most of the conversations that I hear between young Black men are about violence or are violent in nature. Yet violence is not their disposition. There are some who are approachable and receptive to knowledge and positive change. When possible, we have to talk to them, to teach them that such sinister thinking is commensurate to the malignant ideology of the slave master in eliminating our own race. The ideal that we are enemies of one another is nothing but chicanery.

Let's be real about this. Black men, specifically young Black men, are believed to be incorrigible—a pariah in society. This isn't to be brushed off, looked over, or laughed at. THIS IS SERIOUS!

Averting blame to the epoch of slavery or pseudo-white supremacy will not suffice. This is our fault, our responsibility; it's time to be accountable. These are our children, and this is our fight.

What part are you willing to play in revolutionizing the Black community, in educating our children, and in helping to stop this Black-on-Black violence?

In order to counter the centuries of t hepsychological raping of our youth, we must teach them their true identity—who they really are, not what society, music and movies has told them they are. Teach them to rec-ognize that they have a purpose; help them to see why God gave them the gift of life. They have been taught what to think; we must teach them how to think.

In my opinion, from what I have deduced in observing and interacting with the youth here in prison with me, is when we teach them who they really are, we must be the examples of what we teach. We must teach them where they have come from, to know their ancestral history, problem-solving skills and so on. The violence will begin to dissipate, making our neighborhoods, schools, parks, and communities safer. This is only the beginning.

In my heart, I know that little Black boys and girls are worth loving, and they are certainly worth saving.

LOVE THYSELF AND KIN

"If someone says, 'I love God,' and he hates his brother, he is a liar; for he who does not love his brother, whom he has seen, how can he love God whom he has not seen? And this commandment we have from him; that He who loves God must love his brother. You shall love your neighbor as yourself."

-*1 John 4:20-21; Matthew 22:39*

The Bible tells us that we are to love God with all our heart. He made us in His image and likeness, and we are to love our neighbor as ourselves. I know many don't believe this, but does it seem so hard to do?

To love our neighbor as we love ourselves is very important. When you love yourself, you will not hurt yourself, and you will not allow yourself to go hungry. If you get sick, you will do what you must to make yourself well. So, if we love our neighbor like that, how much different do you think our world would be?

Our failure has come from not loving God, because if we loved God, we would love ourselves and our kin. Being separated from the love of the Father has caused us to detach from self. God did not separate his love from us, but we separated from Him, and by doing so, we have allowed a hatred of self and kin to take root. Look at how we treat one another, how we talk to and look down on one another.

We have all known someone or a group of people that we didn't like. I know that I have said that I don't like someone. I hear younger guys say it all the time, and ladies, now ya'll know that ya'll have some other female that ya'll claim to not like.

I have thought about this and have come to the conclusion that it is nonsense. Most times when a person expresses dislike for someone, there is no real reason for it. So, when I hear someone say they don't like someone else, I ask them to be honest with themselves and tell me what legitimate reason they have to not like the person; 90% of the time, there is no answer.

I am not a therapist or a licensed counselor yet, but for me or anyone else to dislike someone without a valid reason means there is an internal issue that needs to be worked out. It should be evident that a hatred for others without reason is a reflection of self-hatred.

Why do we not love ourselves as we should? The answer to that question is inside you. We have to look inside ourselves to honestly self-assess to find that answer.

It may be that we have done something in our past that we have not forgiven ourselves for, or we may see something of ourselves in the other person. Whatever the cause may be, only you and God know, but until we face it, we can't fix it.

We must first turn to God in prayer, individually and as a people. "'Come now, let us reason together,' says the Lord" (Isaiah 1:18). When we turn to God in earnest, He will turn to us and open up our hearts. Then and only then can we honestly inventory our own lives, searching for the root cause of the self-hatred of ourselves and our kind.

Healing begins here!

Every morning, we need to wake up and thank God for allowing us to live another day. We have another day to love our self and kin, to be better than we were the day before. So many lay down to slumber just as we did but did not wake up on this side the next morning.

Each time we look into a mirror, we should tell that person looking back at us how beautiful or handsome they are. Tell them that you love them. If there is doubt, it will deteriorate over time. The more we pray, seek God and encourage ourselves, the more confident we will be and the more we will believe in and love ourselves.

Love is a verb! Love is action! "For God so loved the world that He gave His only begotten Son" (John 3:16). The key to that is" He gave" to show His love for the world.

As we continue looking into that mirror, encouraging and loving ourselves, the reflection starts to look like our brothers, sisters, neighbors our kindred. When love is inside you, it can't be contained. You will have to express that love somehow.

Have you ever been in love? Did you do things to show the other person how much you loved them? Sure you did! Because just to say," I love you," was not enough to show them just how you felt about them.

How about you, mothers, when you gave birth? The moment when you first saw that child, you thanked God for that most precious gift and in that moment, you loved that child more than anyone, more than you love yourself. You show your love for that child by caring for, nurturing, feeding and protecting them. This is the love that God shows us, that we are to reflect back at him and to our brothers and sisters and to our own kind. When true love radiates from someone, it becomes contagious.

Brother George Jackson said this in one of his letters in the book *Soledad Brothers*, "Can you see the division among us and its effect? This is our greatest obstacle.... Before we can ever effectively face down the foe, we must have had long since learned to share, trust, communicate and live harmoniously with each other."

Brother Jackson also said, "To share, trust, communicate, and live harmoniously with each other ," is what is needed for our survival and advancement. It takes love of self and kind. These are the fruits of that love, and when expressed, no one can deny it or destroy it.

There should never be a question as to whether we are loved by our own kind. When we want the best for one another, and when we are willing to help each other set and achieve goals, and encourage one another along the way, this should be a clear enough answer as to our love for one another.

It must be understood that if one of us succeeds and we reach back to help another, then we can all succeed.

Just as we love ourselves, and will fight to save our own lives, if we are taught to love our kind, then we will fight to save their lives as well.

The cold hard truth is that we are not in this world alone. We have a family of people who look just like us. It may be that we are shaded differently, or we may be shorter, taller, slimmer, thicker, or whatever the case may be, but one thing can't be denied: we are all one family.

If animals can care for and show love or concern toward their own kind, shouldn't we also be able too? There was an incident where a dog was hit by a car while trying to cross a busy highway with some other dogs. The other dogs had already made it across the highway, but the dog that got hit was timid and afraid to cross. On the other side of the highway the dogs waited for their companion, seemingly encouraging him to come on across. When the frightened dog finally made the attempt to cross the highway, he was hit by a car, and when the other dogs saw what had happened, they all ran out, stopping traffic and mak-ing sure that the hit dog made it out of the highway safely.

Thankfully, the dog survived with non-life-threat-ening injuries, but the moral to this story is this: if dogs or any animal with nowhere near the intelligence of a human, like you and I, can love and care for their own kind and see to their well-being, how much more should we love our own kind, THE BLACK RACE?

"He who does not practice righteousness is not of God, nor is he who does not love his brother. For this is the message that you have heard from the beginning, that we should love one another... By this we know love, because He laid down His life for us. So we ought to lay down our lives for the brethren (our kind), but whoever has this world's goods, and sees his brother in need and shuts up his heart from him, how does the love of God abide in him? My little children; let us not love in word or in tongue but indeed and truth" (1JOHN 3:10-11; 16-18).

Love of self and kind will most assuredly help us to stop the violence and make advancements as a people.

EDUCATION

"We want education for our people that exposes the true

nature of this decadent American society. We want education that teaches us our true history and our role in the present day society."

-Black Panther Party, Ten-Point Program

Education is one of, the most important elements of the growth, economic development, and civil advancement of a race and a society.

Education is a continual process. It begins in the womb and ends with death.

The womb is a cocoon, an incubator in which the child inside of it is developing in so many ways, and the greatest muscle we have, the brain, is also developing. Therefore, it is very important that we begin to shape their minds from that point. How you say? By taking time to read a variety of materials to them every day. Things such as fun children's books, educational books, stories, history, educational games, etc.

Now I'm no expert, so I can't guarantee that this method works, but who's to say it doesn't? Babies are very intelligent.

When the child is born, we are to continue daily readings, because at this point, we know for sure that the child's brain is acting, reacting and absorbing everything. Along with the daily readings, talk to them, and show them pictures, explaining to them what they depict, and play audios of books to them. Yeah, it may be a one-sided conversation when you are talking to them, for now, but that is the art of teaching. Plus, when they do start talking, you won't be able to get a word in. As they grow, they will pose questions to you that you may not have answers to.

I heard a commercial on the radio about a pre-school. I won't mention its name here, but the services it provides in educating our children and preparing them for kindergarten is our job as parents.

We are our children's primary educators, and as such, we are responsible for teaching them how to spell their names, count, teach them shapes, the alphabet, and colors. We are to teach them of their true history; our children should be able to identify with who they really are and their ancestral history to better understand their roles and responsibilities toward their families, peers, and community.

The emphasis on ancestral history will embed in their minds and hearts just how important they are. That their Black is most certainly beautiful, and that they are descendants of kings, queens, emperors, empresses, and great rulers of mankind. They will know that aside from slavery, our ancestors were architects who built and civilized nations; they were great thinkers and social innovators. We must teach them that our ancestors were the founders of science, astrology, astronomy, mathematics, engineering, technology, arts, and literature.

The true teaching of our great and rich history and culture will help to build a confidence in our children, a love for themselves and for those who look like them, to give them hope and a bond that can never be broken.

The real, public institutions of education are not for the proper teaching and advancement of people of color. They're not teaching our children our way of life, nor what they need to excel in today's society.

Look to history for the truth of today, like what Senator Henry Berry said in 1832 WHEN addressing the Virginia House of Delegates. "We have extinguished every avenue by which light could enter into the mind of the Black slave. If we could extinguish their capacity to see the light, our work would be complete. They would then be on a level with the beast of the field; and we would be safe. I am not certain that we would not do it, if we could find out the process; and that on the plea of necessity."

Upon graduation from public high schools, especially here in the South, Black kids are not actually college-ready. They do not have the substantial science, economics, math, art and technology programs needed to enter the growing job markets in those fields.

Here in the city of Birmingham, Alabama, public schools are failing. It is no secret, yet the first thing on the Alabama legislature's agenda in 2017 is to vote on giving the governor and Department of Corrections $800 million dollars to build four new prisons. Yeah, that's right; even with failing schools, they are more concerned about allocating funds to the Department of Corrections for "PRISONS" than to education.

Public schools are underperforming, and our children are being disproportionately expelled and having police called on them for something back in the day you'd go to the principal's office for.

They have to make sure they keep the school-to-prison pipeline running. These people do not care whether our children are properly educated or actually educated at all. They are into making profits, and placing our children in prison is how they make their profits.

Take this excerpt from The Making of a Slave by Willie Lynch: "For example, you take a slave, if you teach him all about your language (economics, science, technology, politics, etc.), he will know all your secrets, and he is then no slave, for you can't fool him any longer, and being a fool is one of the basic ingredients to the slavery system."

I know a lot of people will say, "Oh man, we not in slavery no more!" Although that is true, if we are not properly educated, we can be fooled. Thus, we become psychologically and economically enslaved.

It is conducive to our advancement that we educate and re-educate our children and people. We need many more Black doctors, surgeons, chemists, scientists, and political leaders with our best interest as a race of people at heart. There will never be enough biologists, astrologists, judges, lawyers, caregivers, educators, etc. of color.

Our mission is to obtain the knowledge and use that knowledge to help build up our communities. In order to change the way in which our children and our people view themselves and the world at large, we must bombard them with intelligent speakers, educators, and leaders, who look just like them. People they will all grow to love, trust, respect, and try to be as they are or better. Watching them work, seeing what it produces, and seeing the fruits of their labor. Being able to see the wide range of contributions to minor and major industries will feed the need of our youth to thrive and also to make great contributions to our communities themselves.

I know that I am not alone in believing that the better educated our youth are, the more opportunities they will have and the less violent they will be toward one another.

As we teach our children to identify with who they really are and not who society says they are, and as we teach them that their mental capabilities has no limit, then by their actions individually and collectively, they will have the power to not only change their reality and their community, but they will have the power to change the world.

"A wise man will hear and increase learning.... Happy is the man who finds wisdom, and the man who gains understanding.... The Lord by wisdom founded the Earth; by understanding He established the heavens.... Wisdom is the principle thing; therefore get wisdom, and in all your getting get understanding" (Proverbs 1:5, 3:13, 19:4-7).

This is the wise counsel of Solomon who knew that the foundation of knowledge and wisdom is God.

Therefore, let us educate our children that they may be wise in our absence. That they may excel from generation to generation for hundreds and thousands of years to come.

BLACK MONEY POWER

How do we obtain a meaningful, stable and strong position, a voice not ignored in this society? UNITY! Financial, intellectual and spiritual unity equals economic growth. We are one body of people, the Black man in America. It don't matter your social or financial status; you are a part of the Black community. You Black, ain't ya?

As a nation of people, Black people, we have so much power as a consumer. The only problem for us is that we spend from 90 to 94% of our money outside of our own communities and business and on frivolous material possessions.

We spend so much time hustling to make it out of the hood that when we finally make that major move, or get that big break, we tend to forget about the very place and people who gave us life. We forget about those who, now that you've made it, need to learn the blueprint so they can make it also. We are not investing in our own communities as we should.

A little charity here, a fundraiser there, a smile for the camera and we good, right? It is these people, us living in poverty, who make the Black celebrity rich. The charities and fundraisers are good things, but they are not sufficient enough to make our quality of life better. We need real investments.

The collective buying power of Blacks in America is $1.3 trillion dollars. Not million or billion but trillion. Now that is a lot of money, but what good does it do us when the bulk of that is spent outside of the Black community and not reinvested back into Black-owned businesses?

With this type of buying power, just imagine what could happen if we would invest all of that or fifty percent of it back into our own businesses and communities. That would mean greater job opportunities for Blacks, the ability to invest in a better educational system of our own, job training, and a higher standard of living for us all.

Today, Blacks own 2.6 million businesses in America. It should be our objective to double or even triple that number as rapidly as possible, reinvesting our profits into more businesses, real estate, farms, food distribution and processing facilities, ports, and Black media. By doing so, it would eventually mean economic independence for us, and that is what we need.

When we begin to collectively invest our money into such ventures, buying complete or majority ownership in corporations, we will then have a louder voice and a stronger pair of legs to stand on, and arms that cannot so easily be pushed aside in politics and in corporate America.

The median household of Whites own 13X more wealth than Black households. That number has grown since 1983 when the White-Black wealth gap was 8x more. Looking at then and now, we have to ask ourselves, how is this possible? How are we steadily falling behind when we should be moving forward and advancing economically? The answer is simple. We spend most of our money on material possessions of no value so we can look good for the moment, and we tend to live above our means, when we need to save or invest in stocks or valuable assets that will generate wealth that can be passed on to the next generation.

Check this out! The Walton's, the family who owns Wal-Mart, possesses more wealth than 40% of Americans, and probably 90% of Black Americans; that is more than 53 million American households.

You think that's something? Approximately eighty people own or possess more wealth than 3 billion people worldwide, and 8 of those people, all billionaires, are Americans.

Walmart is the most frequented shopping center for the Black consumer, but how much of that wealth are they investing back into the Black community?

We have the power to start our own Black-Mart, by us for all. Marketing and selling to all consumers and benefiting the Black community. We have the power to raise the Black employment rate, stop the violence, promote, teach, provide higher, better education, and encourage entrepreneurship in Black communities. We can end poverty or at least knock a major dent in it.

Did you know that a dollar circulates in the Black community for just six hours, and only two cents of every dollar a Black person spends goes to Black-owned businesses? What if that dollar circulated longer? What if, instead of two cents, Black people spent ten or twenty cents of every dollar with Black-owned businesses. What enormous economic growth that would bring to Black communities everywhere. Imagine the possibilities.

Research shows that if higher income Black consumers would spend at least $1.00 of every $10.00 with Black-owned businesses, it would generate 1 million jobs for Black people. So why not spend $2, 3, 4, dollars of every $10.00 in Black-owned businesses? This shows us that we have the power but lack the accountability.

What saddens and sickens me is how we have conformed to the attitude that we'd rather spend our money in White, Asian, Italian, Jewish and Mexican America, instead of Black America. They have their businesses on every corner of our neighborhoods, but they ain't investing any of the money we spend with them back into our neighborhood.

We should depend on one another, but the mind of self-sufficiency we have been divested of. So now we throw all our money away, and then look to others and beg for a handout like someone owes us something. Why do we need outside help when we can help ourselves? But first we need to reshape our thinking. We have this absurd idea that we don't want to spend our money with our own people for fear they may be living better than us. Such misguided thinking! When we spend all our money with every other group of people, they live and eat better than us.

How foolish is this? We want to dress in high fashion and drive cars we can't afford, while owning nothing and having nothing.

Look at how banks and lending institutions do us. How they either will not make loans to us or they give us high interest loans that we can't afford. By the time you pay these loans back in full, you have paid double what the original loan amount was.

But if we were to invest in our own banks and lending institutions, then we could get low-interest loans. We could buy up those abandoned homes and vacant lots in our neighborhoods before the outside investors come in and buy up land and property, forcing us out and raising rent to where we can't pay it.

Investing in Black communities means investing in self. It does not matter that you don't live in the hood. You got family in the hood. But if you are Black, whether you accept it or not, you are part of the Black community. Unless you can turn yourself White or other, there is no exclusions for you.

With those abandoned homes, we can remodel them creating homes for poor families in our communities, childcare, or learning centers. Vacant lots can be parks for children, the elderly, and disabled or turned into community gardens. In the long run, gardens will save families money and produce an income to be reinvested. Plus, with community gardens, we'd know what was in the fruits and vegetables. Not to mention the health benefits. The same is true with investing in farms and livestock.

It is of the highest importance that we start depending on our own for employment, education, healthcare, food, shelter, clothing, etc.

If we, the Black community, do not care about our economic, social, educational, technological, health, political well-being, stability, and advancement, then who do we actually think will care?

BLACK LIVES MATTER/ALL LIVES MATTER

"We are at a tipping point for major change. These senseless killings are outrageous and unacceptable. It's like a slap in the face. It is a constant reminder that our lives-our Black lives- are literally meaningless."

-Alicia Keys

I'll start this chapter by paying respect to the many brothers and sisters that have lost their lives to thoughtless, unnecessary violence. May they all rest in peace, and I pray that God comforts their families, loved ones, and friends.

Tamir Rice, Oscar Grant, Jordan Davis, Treyvon Martin, Darren Hunt-Williams, Rekia Boyd, Mike Brown, Corey Bell, my childhood friend and schoolmate, Jonathan "MOP TOP" Sanders, Ashaunti Butler, Sandra Bland, La'Niyah Miller, Eric Garner, Dominique Battle, Sean Bell, Andy Lopez, Amadou Diallo, Terrence Crutcher, Freddie Gray, Alex Nieto, Antison Shum-pert, Mario Woods, Alton Sterling, Donte Hamilton, Philando Castile, Sky Mockabee, Jessica Williams, Korryn Gaines, Mark Essex, Anthony "Kima" White, Zayd Shakur, Frank Fields, and LaQuan McDonald, who was shot 16 times by the Chicago Police Depart-ment in 2016, and the countless number of those I have not named.

Not one of these people should have lost their lives by the hands of the very people who were hired to protect and serve them. The police are not hired to protect only a certain demographic. They are hired to protect all people.

The loss of these Black men and women was not only devastating to their families and communities, but Black communities all across America were also devastated.

Any time a Black person, a person of color, or anyone is killed by the police, it is tragic and frightening, especially when it is found out that they were unarmed, and the police were unprovoked. When this happens, it is certainly a time to protest, to stand in solidarity for justice and to say that we will not stand for this kind of treatment.

Well, what about the little Black girls and boys and the Black youth who are being killed and killing one another in Black communities all over America every day? Why have they not made national news? Why is there no one speaking up for them? Why is there no protest, rally, march, and justice seeking for them? Do we not care for them? Are we saying that it is okay for Black youth and Black men to kill one another? What is the message?

This comment by Alicia Keys resonates with me because it is the truth: "These senseless killings are outrageous an unacceptable." Although she was talking about the police killings of unarmed Blacks, it is also very true among us. But it seems that no one wants to focus on the Black-on-Black violence issue. Well, it sure ain't gonna stop until we put a stop to it. Our children are dying in record numbers, and it looks like it's not slowing down. And they are being killed younger and younger.

In 2016 in Birmingham, Al., not a large city, there were over one hundred murders, and in Chicago, there were over seven hundred murders. That is a lot of murders for just two cities and 95% of the victims were Black and brown men of color and their killers looked just like them.

We should all know and understand that Black lives matter, just as all lives matter, but if Black lives don't matter to Black people all day, every day, constantly, if it only moves us and brings us together when a Black person is killed by the police or some angry white person but not when a Black person kills, robs, rapes, assaults, and harms in any way another Black person, then Black lives really don't matter.

The same way that we come together and are outraged when we feel that one of our people has been done wrong by the system, we have an obligation to do the same and more when we wrong and when we harm one another.

As a people, a community, and a village, we are to love, care for, educate, encourage, and empower each other. It is a fact that our children cannot safely play outside. They can't enjoy a balanced, happy life without being able to play outside and feel safe. This is detrimental to their psychological and physical development. But when crime happens in our communities, we get deaf, dumb, and blind. That is until crime comes knocking on our door.

If the police calls you to identify the body of your child, or if you are called to the scene of a crime where someone you love is lying in a puddle of blood filled with bullet holes, "STOP SNITCHIN" will mean nothing to you. You will want all the answers you can get.

When my little brother James Davis was killed in 2007 inside of a slum in Prichard, Alabama (Alabama Village), the police were trying to find out what had happened. When they tried to question a bystander, his response was, "I don't know nothing, man. Don't ask me nothing. I have to live here, I can't tell you nothing." Not that he didn't know anything; he just couldn't "tell nothing." This message let other young Black men know that it is okay to kill one another. No one really cares.

This kind of attitude says that we are living in fear, and that is foolish. It is foolish because if we think that we are keeping our children safe, and our communities safe by not speaking up, then that makes us fools. Black neighborhoods are war zones, and we are our own enemies and our children are the casualties.

If any of this sounds crazy to you, how can you say that Black lives matter? When we say that Black lives matter, then that means we want Black people to live. We want to see Blacks prosper and be happy. This means that we don't turn a blind eye, a deaf ear, and lose our tongues when it comes to the Black lives and issues around us.

George Jackson said, "Love of self and kind is the first law of Nature." That sound bout right to you?

Shouldn't you love yourself? If you are Black and you love your Blackness, shouldn't you also love your own people?

Do Black lives matter?

We are burying Blacks rapidly, even children who have not had the chance to taste the goodness of life. Why? Because many of them can't control their emotions. Because they have not been taught how to think, and because they don't have respect for human life.

We'll say, "I ain't got nothing to do with that; it ain't none of my business as long as it ain't nobody in my family." That sounds really familiar, huh? But guess what, we are all family. Our ancestors were used like stud horses to breed from one plantation to another. Just think about that.

If Black lives matter, and they do, to whom do they matter? Is it that Black lives only matter to Black people in certain situations? Black lives can't matter to Blacks all the time, because if they did, we would constantly be in neighborhoods marching and protesting all the "senseless, outrageous, unacceptable killings" of Blacks by Blacks until it stops. We the community have the power to do that. Not the police and not the government, but all of us together.

All lives matter because Black lives matter, and Black lives matter because all lives matter. The million-dollar question is, when will Black lives matter to Black people?

When a Black life is taken, the Black community should and must be outraged and take immediate action.

Blacks are a pariah in America. We are looked upon as scapegraces. But we can thrive in unity. All it takes is for us to love, respect, be responsible, accountable, and encourage one another. Then no one will be able to stop our growth or prosperity.

The only reason the police kill us, thinking it is okay and they can get away with it, that no one cares, is because we have been depicted as miscreants, vilified by all media for decades and the way we have been toward one another, that it seems that we don't care about ourselves as a people.

How do we make Black lives matter to all people? How do we change the view of a society toward a people to whom they deem incorrigible? I'll tell you how! By making Black lives matter to Black people. Not just when it feels good but all the time.

I suppose the ultimate question is, what are you willing and ready to do? What sacrifices are you ready to make to ensure that your children's lives, your grandchildren's lives, that all lives, but most assuredly, that Black lives matter!

LOVE

"Owe no one anything except to love one another, for he who

loves another has fulfilled the Law."

-Romans 13:8

Love is a common denominator. Everyone wants to love someone and be loved by someone. Without love, nothing will work. Discipline does not work without love. This four letter word is what is missing in our world. People throw it around with no meaning and no emphasis to it. "I love you!" To so many, those are just words. I hear young brothers say it to one another: "I love you, bra," but they don't mean it because they will turn right around and steal from, rob, cheat, talk about, and even kill that same person whom they just told they love. Why is this though?

If you were told throughout your life, "I love you," but were treated badly and never shown how love looks in action, then how can you know how to give love or even receive love, when you don't know what love looks like? "By this we know love, because He laid down His life for us. And we also ought to lay down our lives for the brethren" (1 John 3:16).

That being said, why do we harm our children by subjecting them to things that are not good for them?

"Love does no harm..." (Romans 13:10). We allow them to partake in that which we know is not good for them. We know they are headed in the wrong direction, yet we say that we love them and do nothing to stop them. "My son, do not despise the chastening of the Lord, nor detest His correction; for whom the Lord loves He corrects. Just as a father the son in whom he delights" (Proverbs 3:11-12).

Look at what this says, "The Lord corrects who he loves, just as a father his son," so if we say that we love our children, shouldn't we correct them instead of letting them go their own way to destruction? "God has not given us a spirit of fear but of power and love..." (2 Timothy 1:7).

Love is a verb. When you love, you take action. I was listening to a local talk radio show, the Joe Lockett Show, and on this day, they were talking about a young man named Javaris Webb, who was gunned down on his way home from school. He was someone's baby, only 17 years old. On the show, there were some other teen's present; one was a young Black male named Logan, 18 years old. Mr. Lockett asked Logan, "What do ya'll need from us, parents and adults?" Logan responded through tear-filled emotions one word, "Love!" Our youth and our children need to be shown love.

It is not their fault that they are the way they are. They are that way because we allowed the. To become so; we made them that way. We stopped showing them love and started loving material possessions more than we loved them. We love our cars, clothes, jobs, jewelry, money, boyfriend or girlfriend more than we love our children. "You yourselves are taught by God to love one another" (1 Thessalonians 4:9). We are not to love material things.

How can children commit crimes and kill with no remorse? It's because they don't know love. A young brother confided in me one day. He committed murder when he was only 17 years old. He said that what he missed in life was genuine love from his parents; his dad failed to love him. He said that one day, while he was in his room on the phone, his dad came in and told him to fold up some clothes that were lying around. When he did not get right up and do it, his dad came back into the room and said, "So you not going to fold the clothes." That led to a small disagreement, but he said that while they were arguing, he said that his dad said, "Well I see that I can't buy your love," and that, he said, pushed him over the edge.

We should never, ever say or imply to our children that we are trying to buy their love, not even when joking. A child's love cannot be bought. It has to be earned. We earn their love by loving them first, genuinely and unconditionally. "Let all that you do be done with love" (1 Corinthians 16:19).

"Greater love has no man than this, than to lay down one's life for his friends" (John 15:13). We should not only live for our children, our family, and our friends, but we should also be willing to die for them that they may live a better life.

Medger Evers, Marcus Garvey, Martin Luther King Jr., Malcom X, Harriet Tubman, Sojourner Truth, Stokely Carmichael, Huey P. Newton, Bobby Seale and many more loved, fought, protested, marched and died for the love they had for their people.

"But the fruit of the spirit is love" (Galatians 5:22).

Do we love ourselves? Do we love our children? Do we love our spouses? Do we love our parents? If we answer unequivocally yes, then we must be ready to make the ultimate sacrifice and to show through our actions how we love.

There can be no revolutionary change if there is no love.

This is love: "Love suffers long and is kind; love does not envy; love does not parade itself, is not puffed up; does not behave rudely, does not seek its own, is not provoked, thinks no evil; does not rejoice in iniquity, but rejoices in truth; bears all things, hopes all things; endures all things. Love never fails" (1Corinthians 13:4-8).

Love one another to no end, because in love, we cannot fail.

"Above all things, have fervent love for one another, for love will cover a multitude of sins."

Real, true, genuine love will change things.

CONCLUSION

"If we want to lead the people, we must not be out of their sight."

-Sojourner Truth

The only way a real revolutionary change can take place in the Black community is for us, Black people everywhere, to be ready and willing to make that change happen.

The love that our ancestors had for their people, family, friends and neighbors is the same type of love that we must practice. They fought, marched, were lynched, burned, bombed, and sacrificed all. Not for selfish reasons but so that future generations and their children could have a better life than what they had experienced.

What our ancestors did, the way the village worked together to raise the children, is how they made sure everyone had food, shelter, and clothing and were healthy. We must bring back those old ways. Children had respect for parents, adults, and elders. Violence and murders were not common, and kids could explore the outdoors freely and safely. Yeah, I know, we past that right? But just admit to the fact that it worked. We can get back to that, but to do so, we need to make a lot of changes and many sacrifices.

We are so caught up in material things and trying to get money at any cost, that all of our focus, our attention is on material possessions. We have forgotten about raising our children. We have allowed them to be raised and guided by the streets, music, movies, and false propaganda. They don't know whether we love them or not. They don't even know what love is. Where is the love? In material possessions, new fashion, Jordans, gold, diamonds, hair, nails, social status, or Facebook likes? Not at all!

Those are all distractions just to stop our progress and cause strife between us. This from the secret cov-enant tells the truth of it, "We will focus their atten-tion toward money and material goods so they may never connect with their inner self. We will distract them with fornication, external pleasures and games so they may never be one with the oneness of it all. Their minds will belong to us and they will do as we say. If they refuse, we will find ways to implement mind-altering technology into their lives."

Well, take an opened-eye look around you and what do you see? I see a well thought-out plan working, but the good thing is that we ain't all asleep. None of the material goods makes us happy inside and it doesn't matter how much we have; it's never enough. Money will not solve our problems; they run much deeper than that.

I know that many will say that it's out of hand now, and we can't regain control of those youngsters; they will kill you. They are too wild; they don't care for no one. Well, I believe otherwise, and if need be, I am willing to sacrifice my life to prove it, because the same thing was said about me once by my own family—people that I would die for without ever thinking about it.

Many think that people can't change. Well, I'm living proof because now I don't want to die for anyone. I want to live for everyone. Muhammed Ali said,

"Impossible is just a big word thrown around by small men who find it easier to live in the world they've been given, than to explore the power they have to change it. Impossible is not a fact. It is a declaration. It is a dare. Impossible is potential. Impossible is temporary. Impossible is nothing."

If we put our trust and faith in God, if we obey His commandments individually and as a unit, then change will come. All of us may not live to see it, but it will come.

"Will you not revive us again, that your people may rejoice in you? Show us your mercy Lord, and grant us your salvation. I will hear what God the Lord will speak, for He will speak peace to His people and to His saints; but let them not turn back to folly" (Proverbs 85:6-8).

With a heart of love, let us do the work that is set before us, together. I dare you to help make what they say is impossible, possible. Let's you and I make it possible.

"We must walk by faith and not by sight"
(2 Co-rinthians 5:7).

AUTHOR'S NOTE

Ight, I ain't gonna beat around the bush. I have no degrees or certificates nor any prestigious name or title. Not yet! Although, to have a name or title makes no difference to me. Eventually, I will have degrees and certificates. My circumstances just won't allow it at the moment. What I do possess are life experiences that a degree can't provide, as well as personal obser-vations, passion and compassion for our youth and our people.

When I put this pen to paper, the words come from deep within my soul. I am giving of myself all that my circumstances will allow. But this is only the beginning!

I pray that what I write will touch the hearts, souls and minds of the readers. I aim to provoke thought that will encourage and empower change and set forth action!

From what I observe here daily inside these prison walls, and from what I hear on the news and talk radio shows, there is a need for revolutionary change in our youth and in our communities. The way in which we teach our children must be changed. Being and setting a great example is of the gravest importance.

We must love, not in word only, but indeed and truth, making all necessary sacrifices to save our youth, to save our communities, to save our people. What will happen to our future generations? DO WE EVEN CARE?

I KNOW THAT I DO!